PERFECTING THE ACT OF DROWNING

ERIK BELMER

Instagram: @erikthepoet
Cover Art by Matt Sohl
Instagram: @sohlaroids
Editors: Mikayla Cyr, Blake Foster

ISBN: 9798373977968

Contents

It's not about a fine line between genius and insanity, it's about insanity creating the façade that a line exists between opposites

Erik Belmer

Input

Feed the weak
Fight the strong
Live your life and lead on

It's a battleground of self-denial
Outsource your soul
And make the world whole
Because it needs our input
At least for a little while

Chess

Conversations,
Bleak and meaningless,
Lacking weight,
With a cyclical delirium.

Words become pointless,
Tone becomes understanding,
Not speaking becomes the age.
Ghost walking is our daily,
As you pour your energy,
Fruitlessly.
As you hold your energy,
Furtively.
Defense or offense,
Which words are best?
Situations scream it's all chess!

Walls

The normal abhorrence
Staring at the ceiling
Blanking out in a scenario delirium
Not today...
Blanking out with a profound smile
Positive oscillating coaster of elation
Piano keys in bright chords
Perfection in background music
Eclipsed by her face in the forefront
And everything that might be

For once staring at the walls
Is a positive reflective
Not because you painted the room yellow
Because she painted your mind with expectations
As if hope had a color

What color will she make of dreams

Reanimate

I feel it.
Fading ghost in the room.
I fear words,
For it to come to life.
To raze us to ruin,
Ground level,
Rubble brick and mortar.
Cement dreams.
Feelings locked in place.
If we don't speak,
Can abstract be locked, caged, and irrevocable,
A wind whisper?
Or do all things in concrete eventual reanimate?
What kind of foundation did we build?

Architects don't just build skyscrapers
Some build ideas
Ideas That last a lifetime
Echoing throughout history
Never being torn down

Erik Belmer

Pseudo American Dream

Don't turn the knob
Flip the switch
Remit, return, omit

You're not the future
You're just a creature
Who can't alleviate
A sense of emergency

Time is running out
To fit into the mold
Of the American Dream

Of children
Of family
A steady job
And a woman at home who sees me

I'm the creature
Who wants
Who feels
Who can't walk on his own two feet

How do you make a decision
And pull the trigger
When a future mold escapes your fingers

Maybe it was
Maybe it is
Maybe it was never me

You aren't supposed to fit any mold
You're just supposed to be me

Concrete

What happened to our thoughts?
Where are our dreams?
The sift in an endless eternity.
Skyscrapers and offices,
Held by earths conformity.

You hate your job, your daily,
As you pour your being,
Into the cement that holds the structure.
Your time becomes solidified,
In their ideas, into their progress,
Into an abstract monetary code.
You become a number,
Survival becomes a value.
As you lose the waking light,
Your purpose becomes theirs,
And you become concrete,
Another beam that holds up,
What we were never meant to be.

A vessel,
A pawn,
A sacrifice,
You're worth more than liquid knowledge,
In the vat of human's atrocities.

So, I sit hermit-like,
Idly… with a bottle,
Waiting for the infrastructure to come down.

I'm Still Here

A uniform conformity of humanity
We all have our own hell
Hidden inside our personal shells
You let them in and they walk on out
But look inside the mirror to fix yourself

A cosmic indifference of coping skills
Based upon how much you learn
Just so you don't dwell
On the past negativity that poisons our true selves

Look beyond your tattered future cadaver
And return to what really matters
How to live
How to survive
How to thrive

Suffer, molt, change, recover
It's not the skin of another
That makes us find the love undiscovered

It's learning to hold the hand your given
And say I write my own way of living
I'm not just another victim
Or another catastrophe
How about pure form human gallantry

I'm still here
How about you

Dealer’s Choice

The weaving and waving
Of the unkempt boards
Wet dilapidated up steps
Of futures we can't expect

Fall through or make it up
It's really up to you
The highs or the lows
Which way will you go

It's a clown mirror
Compact or elongated
Make it or break it
Matters what you see

Spirals or straight
Broken or pristine
Termite ridden
Or protected

It's ups and downs
Of a life wound around
A human staircase
There's no escape
You do or you don't

Making your own path
That's the way around
It's hell yes or hell no
Life perspective
The simple unknown

What path will you walk
Approach the tipping point
It's all give and no take

Selfish brain phase

Please don't make a mistake
Stay here and take a stand
Of a life you can't expand
It's do or die with an unentertained mind
You can't rise to anyone's plan
Just accept the dealer’s cards
And play your best hand

Flash Bangs and Sanitizer

Reform doesn't happen idly
And contracts reveal all too late
As humans always take the bait
Expect change and suffer a crueler fate
Those in power would rather have us dance
Dance to our own drum
Thinking we've won
As they write the future
In a document that speaks fate
Except for the invisible ink
That's written in hate
A system that's out of date
Tears us apart during calamity
And guides us all to insanity
Is America really United
No, that happened only once
Now division forces reality
America's well-deserved fatality

Headcase

Time to take a breath
Reinvigorate your soul with music
Sounds that you lost
Drowned out by the bustle
Pierced by dollar sign demands
And corporate mandates

You know that laugh you make
The one when you're by yourself
The smile displayed from memory's recollection

The inward rhythm of accomplishment
Reading a book
Doing the dishes
Finishing that back burner task

The sound of an internal argument
Philosophical in nature
That makes you craft opinions on fact
After you read beyond the media's track

Fall back in love with yourself
Fall back in love with your time
Because the world we created
Doesn't care about your cognitive space
It only cares that the machine runs
And grows
And wins

Once you become another gear
You only belong in one place
Stuck inside the crank case
I say we need another headcase

Old Man in The Sea

Basking in the shroud
Illuminated from a singular yellow ray
Glistening off the water
Hinting of light on an unknown abyss
Your rage dripping into the sea
Churning the beast that summons waves
Crashing upon your grief ridden shores
There's no siren song here
Just the end of oblivion
As you remove another chapter from your mindscape

That was months ago
The moment you let it go
The moment you dropped the body
Your dead husk
Into the sea
Hopefully that waning light didn't reveal
What was never supposed to be

That form is apart from you
Water surging and crashing
Singing the tune
Of the old you
The old angry man in the sea

Chaos Eye

A cold breeze
Sun penetrating two voids
One housing rain with tumultuous anger
The other jet-black clouds and Thor's ire
Basking in the in-between

Your life mirrors
The natural happenstance
The eye of chaos that secludes you
That shapes your emotion
Strips your insecurities
And houses your calm

You sit as nature tears the world apart
Chaos is just a cycle
That sits too close to your heart
It's not your choice
It needs no voice
The world will burn
Grow and renew
It never asked for our point of view

Cycle

It's funny
After people die
They exist more in the mind
In the air carrying conversation
In the absence of their presence
They exist more after not existing
Death making us whole

Erik Belmer

Chameleon

Two lifestyles
Bounty distraught
One with uppers
One with downers
It's all about the drugs
The ones you can afford
The ones you can't afford

Never had to take them
But got to watch
Listen
Observe

We're all fucked
But I can blend in
Wear the suit
Wear the hand-me-downs
Watch the heroin neighbor o.d.
Watch the bank take over a divorced family's dream home
Watch a white privileged dean's list subscription
Watch a fake academic disciplinary probation

Son, you were in the wrong place at the wrong time
Sir ... I've been in the wrong place, the wrong time, my whole life
... Don't think you have any power to change that
...Because I certainly don't

I pissed in the time god's cereal in some other life and now they are seeking judgement in a drawn-out torture

I don't ask for cue cards or false ideals
I was gifted thinking outside the box
Because broken has many more precise pieces than together
And together was never real
Give me the anguish, admonishment and failure
I'll craft your skies, dreams, and words with an ironclad current that will rip your feeble hearts a strewn

Speaking of currents…
The planet is dying
And so are we, every day

At least I know I'll fit in wherever we land
Chameleon was never a choice
Just survival skin

Emotion’s Oblivion

Fuck you universe
For giving me the ability to feel
And fuck you phony prophets
For your doctrine of emotions

A simple mind is pain’s demise
I’m jealous of that blessing
To live uncontrived
I'd swap out my thoughts
For a day or two of oblivion
Just to ignore emotion’s bitter taste

Science hasn't paved that path
I'll just take another drink from my glass
To numb the quelling drums
Of footsteps down a questionable path

Destiny and instincts’ eternal war
Ebb and flow of a conflicted race
Where time leaves only waste
Of those unfit for a marathon pace

We foolish mortals
Believe love exists beyond chemicals
And hormone inductions
The seductive hope projection
Of love, of being whole
Of making something out of nothing

Don’t expect the unexpected
When all we are taught is death and destruction

Assume nothing
Assume nothing
And emotions will have no weight
When you ascend the human mistake

Sober Night of The Week

I ate a couple of tums
I forgot about the time passed
Then drank some old water
Poisoned, I spat it out
After I already ingested enough to kill me
I decided what I must do

Fingers down the throat
Throwing up your dignity
As your paranoia circles the bowl

Who would do that, poison your water?
My roommate, nah too easy to be caught
And why does he want double rent
...Maybe he wants the bigger room?
Myself...sleepwalking??
... Possibly but I haven't done that for a while
But what if... could you kill someone sleepwalking
I'd be the biggest target
Self-loathing subconscious bastard
Trying to take me down the gutter

Poison control's a queued-up number
Waiting until your vision gets blurry
Or your organs become septic
30 minutes, I think I might be fine
An hour ok I can try to sleep now
But how did this happen?

Don't eat tums without liquid
The coating on your tongue mixed with time and old water will taste like poison
It's hard being overly analytical
Bordering on insanity, considering all options
Those demons don't have a bed
Dancing around unabridged in my head

Constant

It's cold outside
The shower's hot
Still, laying down on the porcelain is chilly
To your shoulder blades
Adversely like the warm water on your chest
Gaze readjusted
No light on
But just enough sun peering through
That the ceiling is white and pure
With shadows dancing on edges
Molding light and dark

Is this what it's like to always be in between
I wonder if anyone else feels like this constantly

Mask

I held it dear
I told no one
For trusting is death
But I still fill that void
The empty desolate place
Where emotions die
Where love burns
As a martyr, as a sacrifice
For fears are hidden
Held beneath linguistics
Masked by words

Acceptance

A wraith-like absent touch
Of ghost limbs that used to feel
Past memories are so surreal

I've been maimed
I've been tainted
Through sordid skies
And clouded eyes
I write my life
With stringent ties

Wasted from life
I begged for death
But I'm still here
Wondering what karma god I pissed in the face of
How do I live on with half an arm?
In this world that's so contrived
Of people's selfish lies
How do I live on?

There's quadriplegics that strive
And I can't stop picturing my demise
It's not fair, but I'm weak
I'm not the human link
To bring the broken together
I'm just another lost endeavor

Please don't blame me
For a future I can't see
This is a sad song with a terrible end

...Then I woke from my dream
The weakness I feared
Was me and my insecurities
How do I live,
When so many suffer endlessly?

It's a hard truth to accept
That so many are better
With more deficiencies
Then what you ever planned to be

Stones and Bones

If obsidian could fluoresce
You would see my necklace
Ornate in geometry
Jagged and toothlike in shape
An elegant sharp reminder
Darkness is beautiful
But hurts close to the chest

The hidden hollow part
That unscrews
Like a turnkey of time
Houses my hero's ashes
...Or what was once my hero
Now just brittle bone dust

Dust that still holds memory's weight
Every hero dies
It's just perspective that seals fate

Hero is a child's word
No big picture
Just a visual glamor
Admonishment or acceptance
Hidden flaws and gallant deeds
Heroes and heroines
They are just like you and me

They man that saved your life
Cultivated your morals
Sculpted your conscience
And guided your spirit
Can also be the man
Turning the key
Locking you in genetic strained prison bars
Helixes, villainous and contemptuous
Poisoning the wellspring of your mental fabric

Sometimes
A hero is just a man
Armed with self-loathing
Who bleeds with overwhelming clarity
Who dies with instant regret
A hero's hands are his biggest fail-set

Too much expectation
Not enough remediation
Hero was never the label he wanted
Let's just say he was a man
And he did his very best
Dear father I know you tried
Time to put your hands to rest

Corpse Suit

I'm dying,
Will you die with me?

No, that's not your place,
To comfort the dead.
Especially when they're still living.

Death's Depiction

When I picture my death
Now, after all the other deaths
Falling backwards drunk
Cigarette in the left
Thumb crushed beer in the right
Eyes open sky wide
Your face smiling back as my best
Brick and mortar shatter my neck
Brains popping out on cobblestones
Blood weaving through stony cracks
Down to sea level
The long haul
Down to the depths
Will my blood pass the test
My world monster
I believe you know best

Posthumous

Apparently...
Every great poet becomes famous
...Posthumously
So as my spoiled liver thickens
More seductive, loose women are given
My epinephrine thrills quicken
Chasing death faster and faster
Completely driven

What was the night for?
Other than avoiding the morning marrow of the night before

Erik Belmer

New Steps

Every day, before walking inside
I look at the new stoop
The new porch
The rotting boards
Slowly decaying under every footfall

Every day I picture coming out the door
You standing there ready to knock
Swaying in anticipation
Then jumping into my arms
As if I timed it perfectly
But every day you're never there
And decrepit wood creaks
My new found daily start

That sacrifice was too much
Too difficult
As if nature's wasn't
Creaks become groans

All you had to do was show up...

Driving me insane would have been allowed
All the good and bad days I would have stuck to
But you never wanted to sacrifice
Angry messages from afar
Mind tricks and shitty quips

All you had to do was show up

I would have let you back in
Instead, I'm just stuck saying never again
I walk out the door every day
New steps I'm not sure how to take
Wooden boards deciding whether to quiver
Or just simply break

Boots

Fingernails dig
Boot cuffs padded and sultry
The heel of atrocities
Slam into the forefront

Of steps that can't affront
A daily remedy
Of what's enough

Peeling my fingers into the fabric
I've had enough
Steps mirroring every solemn step

I've had enough
Floor boarded
Mind adorned
I've had enough
As the boots
Silently slip to the floor
These boots I adore

They walk a path
Most are too afraid to endure

Pluviophile

Basking in the sporadic rain
The torrential happenstance
Allowing it to cover your body
Allowing your spirit
To dip, weave and hover
Above your mortal flesh bag

The neighbor rushed inside
As you sipped your beer
You heard the door lock
And you laughed at the picture
He must assume and misunderstand
His house isn't coveted
Nor are his belongings

Just the simple pluviophile pleasure
The cold awareness of drops from above
That remind you of how small we are
...That brings you peace
So, you sit
Soaking up the gift
The unknown essence
That makes you forget
About man-made hands
And futures that cannot stand

Table Rings

Puddles, wet wood, table rings
Not my coffee table
I see your leftover drink
Half empty poses questions
Is this the victim of the poison
Bathroom stricken or on the run to and fro
…Condensation revelation
Puddle escalation
Time… more time… they are gone
…Murder on the bar top!
Wounded soldier's tell tales
I'm anxious of the puddle
As if we all must melt away
Only table rings to tell our stories
Like trees, it's always a rough estimate

As what happened fades
I wonder why you didn't drink
Maybe that's the perspective paralysis
I'm wondering why you didn't finish your drink, not what was better than the drink

Bulleit For Your Heart

Soft tender cursory sensors, you sift over them letting them envelope your taste:
Oak, vanilla, caramel, earthy spice.
You dilate the veins, soak into the skin.
Slowly molding your seductive, feral, poignant layer inside the hive.
Your puppet seduces,
Weaves words,
Accepts the feelings,
And bathes in them.
Hardening the concept of affirmation.

Obstacles present themselves,
Boring male chauvinists,
That know not of love,
Treating your muse,
As their trophy.

So the brown clenches your fists,
And waits ready.
For the oncoming barrage.

Somewhat thwarted by your rage,
By the brown that gives you confidence.

A staggered trot,
Painted red droplets, gently course down your hands.
The snow soaks in,
Venerable, admonished weight.
To be better and worse simultaneously.
Alone, again,
At the house.
...No lass to be found,
Another drink of brown,
...Why swim when you can drown.

Terabytes

Sifting through the refuse
Avoiding the leftovers
Unless you need to feed
A quick snack for the long journey
The weak prey that's also
A mutual sycophant
To your weakness

Laughing at the selfie-only girls
Deterring the fake straightedges
Avoiding the addicts
A game of pictures
A psychological analysis
Of our biggest disgrace
Putting love on a pedestal
With easy access stairs
Saying anyone can find it
And we all deserve it

The human race made a cheat code
Not to win
But to believe we have won

Nothing is that easy
Love isn't that easy
Profiles are the facade
Overpopulation
Overstimulation
You wade through the muck
You skim over the surface
Because everything can be better
But what's better can't be analysis
It can't be found
Programs can't compute
What was before they were around

"You're A Catch"

A small misunderstood fish
In a genetically overstimulated pond
Fused with chemicals and feed
Everyone chooses the bigger
More doped up
More deficient
Based on looks
But if you could see this minnow
Massive in size
Glistening in health
Swimming faster than any
As it courses around the world
Yeah, he's a catch
But no one sees the blur
The paradigm of colors and hues
That no one else can concur
So, he travels around the pond
Jumping from sea to see
Hoping someone catches a true glance
Of what a hidden fish in a big pond
Can actually be

Failed Protection

I took my glass screen protector off
To try and take a picture of us
But the selfie camera is cracked
Like my technological atrocity
I don't like selfies anyway
I liked that picture though

Now the glass screen is smudged
In the light
It represents a sexual female leg
Adjacent to a fish standing upright
Its mouth where its belly would be
It is parallel to the leg
So it can't kiss, maw or maim
So it swims alone
Because it's upright
Who told it that it had choice
That it could venture to land

Fishes are supposed to be of plenty
It just depends on the sea

Cursed and Blessed

It's that time again
I don't know why it started
Or when it chooses to appear
I just know it will always be near
I tried leaving my demons at the door
Alas, it's only a temporary reprieve
Before they creep back in

There is no barrier or safety
A fortified door and plentiful locks
As your shadow splits and takes form
Your enemies are already indoors

These fucking wicked faced chains
Tethering me in frozen space
Will always be snickering up at me
Meld the maleficence with bone
Solder the demons inside
So I can walk again
At my own pace
With more than one face

I'll be your devil
I'll be your saint
Cursed and blessed
Don't fuck with a mess

The traits of the enemy
The traits of morality
Let them in, let them in
Use them, fuse them
And walk again

I'll be your devil
I'll be your saint
Cursed and blessed
Don't fuck with a mess

Beautiful Creatures

Broken
Damaged
Beautiful
Creatures

The female attraction
My endless distraction

Tattered, scarred, elegant souls
I'll drink the whole bowl

Discard
Prim and proper
Fake and hidden

I want
Chaotic and flagrant
Misjudged and vibrant

Every Day

Someone told me the other day
The rarity of my most known trait
Trying in the face of uncertainty
Giving it your best shot
Not giving up on love
That's my thing
No matter how ridiculous
How reckless
How ridiculed
I'm relentless

Time wasted
Chance taken
Pain embroidered on my soul
Someone has to pay the toll
Each person, each piece
Signs a temporary lease
True love is chasing shadows
Timing has to be just right
Except there are no clocks
Feral innate sun dial that speaks fate

I'll drive you around the US
Just to see if we pass the test
I'll fly out
Just to have my heart stepped about
I'll stay when dishes and glasses are thrown my way
Instead of kisses and what if's
I'll bath in your toxic mist
Because In the name of love
I'll try anything
For that true one to stick

Black Teeth

I stopped writing
** I stopped writing dark things
I kept writing
But only my brain held the ink
So, I kept drowning
Swallowing the black dream
My hand won't hold the pen
So, I keep tasting ink

Maybe with black teeth
You will finally see
Dark things aren't just paper dreams

Creation

It started with pictures
It led to tools
Slowly but surely
We progressed
People died over it
Humans murdered for it
Always on opposite sides
Love and ambition

Feral necessity to create
Mixed with brain chemicals
Forming an unbreakable soulful bond
That is love

Feral necessity to survive
Developed into efficiency
Forming an unattainable tier structure
That is status

As both these evolve
We become
More deceitful, more honest
More cunning, more empathetic
Always two sides
Impossible to support love
In the world we created

Time is the hangman
I failed as a romantic
I gave up on love
To try and reach success
Before the relationship succumbed to death
I took the knife
Cut the feelings out of my chest
Showed you the severed strings
And said look... this is best

As they withered away
Not sure if love or ambition was best
Numbly we both agreed
Creation always sides with success
Love always ends up second best

I lost the "E"

Exuberance
Exaltation
Evermore
Elation
Ever…less
Am I the mess?
Erudite
Err-full
Earmarked for distress
I love you
I lost the E

Lov
I don't want to be like the rest

Bloody Footprints

I did it again
The world did it again
Impossible decision
Every other day you flip-flop
Your brain's on fire
Mentality's fabric frays
Thoughts become ideas
Ideas become fears
Fears become all-encompassing
What ifs and question marks
Rationality is the cause
Rebounds of an irate nature
Make a bigger mess
As you play with hearts
As the life blood seeps out
Destiny's diagram is muddled
With bloody footprints

Except we are all dancing in the same room... and so we dance

IT WAS SUPPOSED TO BE ME AND YOU
AGAINST THE WORLD

REALITY IS, IT'S JUST ME AGAINST THE WORLD
WITH YOU AS A PART OF IT

ERIK BELMER

Audio Masochism

I listened to your favorite band
Not their new stuff
Their older more punk based jams
Not their sell out mainstream stuff
Their stuff that makes you jump out of your seat and scream at the top of your lungs

I did it to myself
I listened purposely
Because I'm a masochist
Because I love you
Because I miss you

Time's Drain

The *I love you* texts in the morning
Are starting to kill me
My two-thousand mile crutch
That wrenches my heart every morning
With a rusty cantankerous turn

So sweet, so beautiful, my nourishment
My love
I never thought I wanted to die
Until I met you
Until I was apart from you

That's why death and love hold hands
As they sift in the drain of time's sands

Sour

Plentiful and luscious
As we were
You chose sour
Now I taste the ending
The one I never wanted

Short natured defense
Vile contemptuous and bitter
Your words open my skin
Fresh new wounds to lick
Blood to bleed
Hot resenting rage
It tastes good to have the end

Lately

Reborn.
I write in the morning,
Hungover grasping for water.
Sometimes present,
Some day's location sundered.

My emotions flood back to me,
Eloquent and detailed.
Sharp for a new day,
After the booze permeates through my macabre skin.
After dying the night before,
All over again.

Lackluster

Early morning eyes
Glued together from the night
Another booze ridden carousel
My voice rang out clemency
To myself
To my pulled back muscle
To my pounding headache
To my mental, sucking in negativity
To my emotions replaying an empty dormant sound

Even emotions are lackluster now
Without you

Coffee

I remember
All of them, all their types
Ingrained in consciousness
Why is it that my necessary morning drink
(The thing that gets me up to go)
Is also filled with tormenting memories
We all know caffeine is a hell of a drug
Who knew it was a hot, steamy conflagration
Tongue cauterizing
Devils' playground
That's hard to swallow
That's what necessity is
Hard to swallow, every morning

Knock-Knock

It's your best friend the
Convoluted countenance
The slim but bleak shroud
Coating the day-to-day
Hovering around my sky
Hello my lover
Come in
What form are you today
Savior
Saint
Cursed wench
Comforting Mary
Do I have a choice
You already have the keys
So why knock
Why the mystery
Always a mystery
Master manipulator
Pure poison with legs and ass
Hold me down and tell me
I'm worthy until morning
I'll still be mourning
While you sleep soundly
I'll still be mourning
Not sure yet of your form

Knowledge

You brought my book to a local library
At least you tried to spread the word of me
Accidentally

I wonder about the old school libraries
People's personal studies
The books
The knowledge
The tomes
Once sought after
Now under appreciated
Just waiting to be fingered over

The fact you sold my book to your local library
Makes me wonder
Do I have to date enough women in different cities
To spread literary motion that should have never died
Or will I become dust on the bookshelf
Waiting to be blown

At least I named myself

Opposite Roads

... I’m going to push you away
... I like you
... I love you
I don’t think I’m afraid
I think you deserve better
I think you’re further along
In a different direction
I believe our paths may have crossed
And been intertwined at one time
Somewhere in the maelstrom
Of naked bodies and nights of error
Mistakes unbeknownst
An alternate reality

Here and now
...We missed our time
We try to tie the strings together
But they fray, they unravel
And we are left split
Again

...You’re going to push me away
...You like me
... You love me
I think you’re afraid
…You’re not too good for me
…You’re just too far along
On the opposite road
At least that’s how I felt

We had the wrong antidotes
For the same poison
Arms linked as we drank each other’s
Standing idly
Watching each other’s eyes
Intently, doubtfully, somberly
Withering while we decay

I Love You Lost

Auto correct
Disconnect
Love you most
Love you next
Future's mailbag

Words swirl and twirl
In the silk of our next
...Chapter
Here and forever after

I love you lost

Before was never found
Since you weren't around

I love you lost

In whatever space and time
And in whatever realm
I love you lost

Lost was never a word
When feet touch ground

I love you lost
In whatever is never found
In the remains of the unsound

I love you lost
Only feelings on this battleground

Worthy

I wanted to become the biggest,
Most self-destructive, convoluted mess.
So you could take me back;
So you could take me in.
But if you didn't think my best was enough,
How could my worst be worthy?

Erik Belmer

Falling Out Of Love

What they don’t tell you
When you fall out of love
Is you will have to forget every laugh
All the different smiles
And quirky looks
The tonality of their snarkiness
The stupid jokes that make you shake your head
That look when they wake up not ready to face the day
The glowing eyes of acceptance after you kiss their forehead to make them feel safe
The misconstrued text messages
The disorganized refrigerator with hidden containers of moldy takeout
The guilty cute face made when you reorganize it
The bad tv habits of asking questions rather than watching
The cringe face made that speaks sorry as the tv rewinds

All the things you love
And all the things you love to hate
Will fade

To move on you will rewire your brain
To forget all the things you love
And all the things you love to hate

Eventually there is no love or hate
Just an expressionless blank slate

I sincerely hope your memory of me has a different fate
When forced to move on
There is no room for love or hate
Just an expressionless blank slate

Per-fec-tion

I don't know how to talk about this
I don't know how to write about this
I don't know
Pulling my hair out
Screaming at the sky
Pissing into the fucking wind

You have made me so weak
Because you changed my perspective
And then expected me "to be"
And I was

I did everything
I believed that true love was wrong
I believed love is about accepting imperfection
Then you told me you weren't one hundred percent... on me
Hypocrisy in the form of a six-inch blade
A gut punch of realization
As I hold my intestines
Your intentions
"My subconscious transgressions"
...Perfection...
Per-fec-tion is not a lesson

Heartbreaker

Shattered,
Piecemeal of your before thought,
At your own hands.
This time,
The first time,
You tore off the cape,
And donned the mask.

The most beautiful,
Caring,
Subjective,
Thinking lass.
She opened back up,
As you pushed her through the glass.

Once pristine and clear,
Now stained
With her surprise.
Stained with your remorse.
Stained with your sacrifice.

Your mind slow to the march,
A step behind the drum,
As time commands the orchestra.

As you feebly fawn after another,
Your mind accosting the reasoning,
The knowledge you don't yet adorn.

You become your own adversary.
One heart
After another.
Honesty as your weapon.
You succumb to a lack of feeling,
As you become what plagues you
As you become the heartbreaker.

Character Defamation

I revel in dramatic appearances and
I die for the acting.
I appreciate the incendiary flare
...Until it becomes real
Taken as gossip
Taken out of context.
Before it becomes a blade
Housing teenage-based nightmares.
Emotions rampant and accosted.
Words unfiltered and directed.
For the stab wounds
That litter my back.
The drama represented
With seething tranquility for one
And only one.
That's not drama…
Call her manipulation and malevolence,
Whom did you speak to
That filled your callous mouth
With only negativity?
Words have power, darling.
I've erred and stared at our faults
A species dance.
Where communication loses light,
And becomes an after thought.
Where words become weapons,
Tools to draw the masses.
Get your pitchforks
The monster has entered the act.
Smile bright
Lights! Camera! Action!
I'm your creature horror delight.

Hope (S)wings

If I could say anything
To make this better I would
If I could explain my fears I would
If I could mold the perfect time flux
I would

But I killed us
I ripped out the wings of hope
And made us both crash-land
And delete became the option
An empty text box
With invisible ink
Is written in my hand
Now all you have are questions
When all you deserve are reasons
But honey reasons aren't in season
Even I got burnt on this one
My self-appointed treason

Hourglass

All I attract is chaos in an hourglass shaped bottle
Sweet luscious temptation
Can't help but unfetter the cap
And let it drive me to ruin

Erik Belmer

Rooftop Sight

Black roofing tar etched
Into the lines in your hands
Into your pinioned knees
Skirting the edge of the towel
That caresses her elegant form
Just like how your lips graze hers
Fingers dig into the back of your head
Into your neck
With forceful arousal
As if you could go nowhere
As if you should stay here forever
Sifting forms under a cool summer night
Clouds covering the stars
Just enough to show you a world beyond
As if you have to truly look to see the real picture
With my eyes closed I think I truly see and feel her
Universally fingers tracing lines

Untamed

Silky sweet foam
Cascading with detritus roots
As if organic matter
Could coalesce me
It sifts over the skin
Coating our being
In the salt based principle
What is too sweet is not wanted for long
Like a bad apple I want the arsenic
Seas worthy deteleportation
A normal shell
Give me the port in the storm
Baby, normal is your hell

Reread

I sifted over our texts.
Reread every word.
Analytically,
Sucking up every emotion.
Letting myself glow,
Letting myself smile,
Bathing in the chemistry.
I let you fill me up,
Because your words,
When spoken to me,
Is nectar from the god tree.

Romantic

They look at you
Wonder why you brought another girl
Does he ever stop?
They look at you like you're a whore
The other half like you're a love sick puppy
Realistically you just try more
You fall and give it your all
Every time with failing grace
That's a romantic
They just aren't and never understood the concept to begin with

So I'll be your whores eye judgement
I'll be your blissfully unaware dog
I'll be all your *supposed* mistakes
I'll be your settling sycophant
Realistically
Every time
I'm the guy that gives love another take

Teardrop

I cried
She licked my tears
Spit them out!!
Those aren't for you

Let's make it 7

Some say they have never loved
Some say they always love
One is ignorant
The other selfish

I stand indifferent
I have loved 7 different times
They don't have pieces of my heart
I have sectioned compartments
Hidden away
That house theirs
Maybe that's not moving on

That's why they have rings on their fingers
And house entities of genetics
Because they don't love
Not the way I do

I can honestly say I love them all
All the different forms
I hope they're well
(Even that one, the bad one)
...
...Lovers don't forget
They coalesce
With memories
Lovers learn
Take the good and the bad
And mold them
into a story
Into a lesson

You either love yourself
Or love the story you created
Not trying is simply outdated
Whether woeful and dour
Or elated and blissful

The lines either cross
Or they don't
True lovers hate the world
Then they recommit
Otherwise love would not exist

Windowsill Earrings

Gaze ascending
The sky red and tumultuous
Blue and pristine
Cleft in two

You wanted me here
Torn a-strew
No, I can't believe that's actually you

It's you moving on at all cost
You just couldn’t care
You’re more truth than dare

Ah, but the private moments we shared
Lost to all those that weren't there
Sexual chemistry I haven’t felt for years
Toss it out if you want, but I'll hold it dear
No lies, just moments transcribed
Under covers, you’re still here

Leftover earrings sit on my windowsill
And I wonder what I'm doing here
Caring about a girl
That could never be there

Shortcut

I was cornered
Agitated and panicked
I trapped myself in someone's backyard
Roaming around trying to find an exit
Through hedges and around the side
I was fenced in... literally
Tequila the labyrinth
A random back door
Housing a couch was the centerpiece

Before the cops came for trespassing
I tossed myself over the ledge
I was trying to get home quicker
But the booze was the driver
Hard pavement my lady of the night
Blood slowly trickling down my arms
Poignant rocks my recompense
As my feet screamed at me
Happy Monday
Now my favorite sandals are gone

Poltergeist

Tell them your fears
Your horrors
Your trepidation
So they mimic them
And become your nightmare
This isn't what you wanted?
Honesty has its price

The End

You can avoid it
Dance around its truth
Time spent will unveil one card
The one with hearts
The one of swords
The love you can't keep
That is the four letter curse word

When you leave your caring subject
Douse her with a close of love
She Mutters under her breath
What did you say
Nothing that matters now dear
In the space of time's furrowed brow

Words swirl and twirl
But the suicide king
He holds time now
His card remains
Pristine
Until he moves his hand
Then the color red
Becomes the end

With a K

I've sat
I have listened
To the aching walls of this ancient house

I have bathed
In the cement, on the porch
In the worn wood, on the upper deck

I have slept in the rooms appointed to me
I have heard the other rooms beckon
For my touch, for my aura

I have poured my heart
Into the endless dream

I have traveled the streets
By foot
By machine
By folly
By love

A mile high
Made my lungs revive
As I cursed
As I spat
On the desert wind
On my topography twist

Mountains and glades
Snow and sun
Rain and hail
You my dear
You won

I'm not sure if I'll ever see a brighter sun
But at least I captured my idea in a memory
Sometimes a picture is worth

A thousand suns
That scourge your eyes

What yet is to come
Now out of our control
But now has not unwound
So suns become beacons
To our ultimate demise
At least your arms are wrapped
Wrapped tightly around mine

So sleep sweet
For the road is at our feet
And future prints
Have yet to be

Sun and Moon

I opened my eyes
I felt my lips leave yours slowly
Those star shaped brilliant blues
They looked back
And tilted toward the skyline
In unison, I had also transitioned

The sun was the backdrop
Slowly fleeting
Leaving us another second of warmth
It didn't know its exchange
Lay between our adjacent bodies already

The moon was above
Crescent shaped
A sharp edge
With a body built to cradle
So fitting
As I'm wrapped in your form
And struck by your tongue

You feel like the best decision
You were supposed to be locked away
But isolation forces derision
While longing for another
Makes a perfect revision

To The Other Side

Once I fled,
In any direction,
But the purpose was known.
Here is not now,
And now was before,
But flight of feet,
And sleight of hand,
Has no bounds.
Untethered space,
Here is not known,
And I cannot stay.
To the other side
…To the other side.

Weightless

Into the ether
Into the everlasting ether
Bouts of bedlam
Accrued mental miasma
A thick syrup licked off destiny's back
An acrid anoxic surprise
As you keep falling
As you keep drowning
Into the ether
Into the everlasting ether

About The Poet

Erik Belmer is a poet based out of Portland, Maine. He is a professional bartender that loves inventing cocktails when he isn't using his creativity for poetry. The themes of his work stem from love, heartbreak, self-image and existential questions. He enjoys writing from perspectives outside of his own and using personification and anthropomorphism. This is his second work of poetry following his first book, Cupids Carrying A 45, and can be found on Instagram @erikthepoet.

Made in the USA
Middletown, DE
28 July 2024